AF582740

A 15-Day COURSE on Manifestation

MAGIC UNVEILED

A Journey on Manifesting Your Best Life

GAVIN TRUESTEEL

MAGIC UNVEILED

First edition. October 19, 2024.

ISBN: 979-8230368809

Written by Gavin Truesteel.

Dedication

This book is dedicated to the younger me—The one who dreamed fearlessly, believed without limits, and embraced the magic of possibility.May this journey remind you, and all who read it, that the power to create the life you desire has always been within you. Keep believing, keep dreaming, and never stop manifesting your magic.

Author's Message to Readers:

Dear Reader,

Welcome to a journey that could change your life in the most magical way possible. The concepts I'm about to share with you aren't just theories—they're experiences, lessons, and truths I've discovered along the way. Imagine living in a world where what you dream of can become your reality, where the invisible forces of the universe are your allies in creating an extraordinary life. This book is your guide to tapping into that power.

I've walked this path myself, and now I'm here to help you navigate it. You don't need to have any special skills or knowledge, just an open mind and a willingness to try something new. As you read through these pages, you'll find simple yet profound ways to start creating magic in your own life. This isn't about spells or potions—it's about understanding the natural laws of the universe and how to work with them to manifest the life you truly desire.

Let's embark on this magical journey together.

With warmth and magic,

GAVIN TRUESTEEL

FOREWORD:

Magic isn't just for wizards and witches; it's something that lives within all of us. The word "magic" often brings to mind images of mystical powers and supernatural forces, but what if I told you that magic is real, and it's something you can access in your everyday life? This book is about discovering the magic within you—an extraordinary power that has the potential to transform your life in ways you might not have thought possible.

I didn't always believe in magic. In fact, like many people, I thought the idea was a bit far-fetched. But then I started exploring, experimenting, and gradually, I began to see that the magic wasn't out there in some far-off land—it was right here, inside me, inside all of us. It's in the way we think, the way we feel, and the way we interact with the world around us.

This book is a culmination of what I've learned on my journey—a blend of insights from other writer's teachings and my own experiences. I've condensed the most important lessons into 15 chapters that are easy to understand and practical to apply. You won't find complicated rituals or difficult exercises here; instead, you'll discover simple, yet powerful, ways to start manifesting the life you've always wanted.

As you read, I encourage you to keep an open mind and a willing heart. The magic is real, and it's waiting for you to tap into it.

As you go along with the book, I want you to read one chapter per day and follow the exercises provided in each chapter.

Let's begin.

Table of Contents:

Chapter 1: The Magic Within: Discovering Your Power

When I first heard the word "magic," I imagined something straight out of a fantasy book—wands, spells, and supernatural abilities. But as I grew older and began exploring the world around me, I realized that magic is something much more real, and it's something that exists within each of us. This chapter is all about discovering that magic within you, and understanding that you have the power to create and shape your reality.

Magic, in its simplest form, is the ability to influence the world around you through your thoughts, emotions, and intentions. Think of it like this: every time you focus on something, whether it's a problem or a dream, you're sending energy towards it. That energy has the power to bring about change, and that's where the magic happens.

I remember the first time I experienced this for myself. I was going through a tough time, feeling stuck and uncertain about my future. One day, I decided to try something different. Instead of focusing on what was going wrong, I began to imagine what I wanted to happen. I visualized myself happy, successful, and surrounded by positive experiences. At first, it felt a bit silly, but the more I practiced, the more I noticed small changes happening around me. Things that used to bother me started to fade away, and opportunities I never expected began to appear.

This was my first taste of the magic within, and it completely changed my perspective. I realized that I wasn't just a passive observer in my life—I was an active creator. And the same is true for you.

The key to unlocking your magic is belief. You must believe in your own power, even when it feels like nothing is happening. It's like planting a seed; you can't see what's happening beneath the soil, but that doesn't mean the seed isn't growing. Your thoughts and intentions are like seeds you plant in the universe, and with time, patience, and care, they begin to grow and manifest in your reality.

In this book, we'll explore how to tap into this power by shifting your mindset and focusing on what you truly want. We'll discuss the importance of self-belief, and how to overcome the doubts and fears that often hold us back. After reading this book, you'll have a clear understanding of the magic within you and how to start using it to create the life you desire.

Exercises:

1. **Self-Reflection:** Take a few minutes each day to reflect on your thoughts and emotions. Are they aligned with what you want to create in your life? If not, how can you shift them to be more positive and focused on your desires?

2. **Visualization Practice:** Start practicing visualization by imagining a simple desire—something small but meaningful. Picture it in your mind as if it's already happening. Feel the emotions you would feel if it were real. Do this daily and observe any changes that occur.

3. **Affirmations:** Create a list of affirmations that reinforce your belief in your own power. Repeat them to yourself each day, especially when you feel doubt creeping in.

This is just the beginning of your magical journey. In the next chapter, we'll dive deeper into the power of belief and how it shapes your reality. Remember, the magic is within you, and it's waiting to

be unleashed. All it takes is a little faith and a willingness to explore the possibilities.

Chapter 2: Believing is Seeing: The Power of Belief

One of the most important lessons I've learned on my journey is that belief is the foundation of all magic. It might sound simple, but the way you think and what you believe about yourself and the world around you have a profound impact on your life. This chapter is all about understanding the power of belief and how it can shape your reality.

Have you ever noticed that when you believe something will happen, it often does? This isn't just a coincidence; it's the power of belief in action. When you truly believe in something, you align your thoughts, emotions, and actions with that belief, making it more likely to become a reality. This is why the phrase "believing is seeing" is so powerful—what you believe in your mind, you start to see in your life.

Let me share a personal experience that illustrates this concept. A few years ago, I was facing a big challenge. I had a dream of starting a new project, but I was filled with doubts. I kept thinking, "What if it doesn't work? What if I fail?" These thoughts were holding me back, and no matter how much I wanted to succeed, I couldn't move forward because my beliefs were working against me.

One day, I decided to change my approach. Instead of focusing on my doubts, I started telling myself, "I can do this. I believe in myself and my ability to make this project a success." At first, it felt like I was just trying to convince myself, but over time, something incredible happened. The more I believed in my success, the more confident I became, and soon, opportunities began to appear that I hadn't noticed before. I started meeting people who could help me, and new ideas flowed effortlessly.

This experience taught me that belief isn't just wishful thinking—it's a powerful force that shapes your reality. When you believe in yourself and your dreams, you create a positive energy that attracts the people, resources, and opportunities you need to succeed.

But what if you struggle to believe? What if those negative thoughts keep creeping in? This is something many of us face, especially when we're trying to do something new or challenging. The key is to understand that belief is like a muscle—it gets stronger the more you use it. You might not believe in yourself fully at first, and that's okay. The important thing is to start practicing, even if it feels difficult.

Here's how you can begin to strengthen your belief:

1. Challenge Negative Thoughts: When a negative thought enters your mind, don't just accept it. Ask yourself, "Is this really true? Is there evidence that supports this thought, or is it just a fear?" Often, you'll find that these negative thoughts are just assumptions or fears that don't have any real basis.

2. Surround Yourself with Positivity: The people you spend time with and the content you consume can influence your beliefs. Surround yourself with positive influences—people who believe in you, books that inspire you, and activities that uplift your spirit.

3. Practice Affirmations: Affirmations are positive statements that help reinforce your beliefs. For example, if you're struggling to believe in your ability to succeed, you might say, "I am capable and confident. I believe in my success." Repeat these affirmations daily, especially when you feel doubt creeping in.

4. Visualize Your Success: Spend time each day visualizing yourself achieving your goals. See it in your mind as if it's already happening, and feel the emotions of success. The more vividly you can imagine it, the more your mind will start to believe it's possible.

5. Take Small Steps: Sometimes, the best way to build belief is through action. Start with small steps that move you closer to your goal. Each small success will boost your confidence and reinforce your belief that you can achieve what you set out to do.

As you begin to shift your beliefs, you'll notice changes in your life. Things that once seemed impossible will start to feel within reach. Remember, belief is the foundation of magic. The stronger your belief, the more powerful your ability to create the life you desire.

Exercises:

1. **Belief Inventory**: Write down your current beliefs about yourself and your goals. Are they positive or negative? Identify any limiting beliefs and challenge them. Replace them with empowering beliefs that support your dreams.

2. **Daily Affirmations**: Create a list of affirmations that resonate with you and repeat them every morning and night. Pay attention to how your mindset shifts over time.

3. **Visualization Practice**: Spend 5-10 minutes each day visualizing a specific goal. Imagine it as vividly as possible, including how you would feel, what you would see, and what you would do once it's achieved.

In the next chapter, we'll explore the power of visualization and how you can use your imagination to turn your dreams into reality. Remember, believing is seeing—when you believe in yourself and

your dreams, the universe aligns to help you make them happen. Let's continue this journey together.

Chapter 3: Visualize to Materialize: The Art of Imagination

One of the most powerful tools you possess is your imagination. Your mind is like a canvas, and your thoughts and images are the paintbrushes that shape your reality. In this chapter, we'll dive into the art of visualization—a technique that allows you to use your imagination to turn your dreams into reality. When you visualize, you're not just daydreaming; you're actively creating a blueprint for what you want to experience in life.

Visualization is more than just picturing something in your mind; it's about fully immersing yourself in the experience. It's about seeing, feeling, and believing that what you want is already yours. When you do this, you're sending a clear message to the universe about what you desire, and in turn, the universe begins to align circumstances, people, and opportunities to make it happen.

I remember the first time I truly understood the power of visualization. I was working on a goal that felt completely out of reach. No matter how hard I tried, I couldn't see a way to achieve it. Then, I came across the idea of visualization. At first, I was skeptical. How could imagining something in my mind possibly make it real? But I decided to give it a try.

Every day, I spent a few minutes visualizing my goal. I didn't just see it in my mind—I imagined every detail. I felt the emotions I would feel if it were already happening. I pictured the sights, sounds, and even the smells of that future moment. The more I practiced, the more real it began to feel. And then, something amazing happened. I started noticing opportunities I hadn't seen before. People came into my life who could help me, and things began to fall into place in ways I never expected.

That experience taught me that visualization isn't just a passive exercise—it's an active way of creating your reality. When you visualize, you're training your mind to believe that what you want is possible. And once your mind believes it, your actions and energy start to align with that belief, making it much more likely to manifest in your life.

But visualization isn't just about thinking positively or wishing for something to happen. It's about creating a vivid, sensory-rich image in your mind and believing in it so deeply that it begins to feel real. The more you practice, the more you'll notice that your reality starts to shift to match the images in your mind.

Here's how you can start using visualization to bring your dreams to life:

1. Get Clear on Your Vision: Before you can visualize, you need to know exactly what you want. Take some time to think about your goals and desires. What do you truly want to experience? Be as specific as possible.

2. Create a Vivid Mental Picture: Once you know what you want, start visualizing it in your mind. Close your eyes and imagine it in as much detail as possible. What does it look like? How does it feel? What sounds do you hear? The more senses you can involve, the more powerful your visualization will be.

3. Feel the Emotions: Don't just see your desired outcome—feel it. Imagine the joy, excitement, and satisfaction you would experience if it were already happening. Emotions are a powerful part of the manifestation process because they help to reinforce the belief that what you want is possible.

4. Practice Daily: Visualization is most effective when practiced regularly. Set aside a few minutes each day to focus on your vision. The more you do it, the more natural it will become, and the more likely you are to see results.

5. Take Inspired Action: Visualization alone isn't enough—you also need to take action. Pay attention to any ideas, opportunities, or intuitions that come to you after you visualize. These are often signs from the universe guiding you toward your goal.

6. Stay Open to Possibilities: Sometimes, what you visualize might manifest in ways you didn't expect. Stay open to different possibilities and trust that the universe knows the best way to bring your desires to life.

As you begin to practice visualization, you'll notice subtle shifts in your life. Things that once seemed impossible will start to feel within reach. Opportunities you never noticed before will appear, and you'll find yourself moving closer to your goals with ease.

Exercises:

1. **Vision Board**: Create a vision board by cutting out images, words, and phrases that represent your goals and desires. Place it somewhere you'll see it every day as a reminder to focus on your vision.

2. **Daily Visualization Practice**: Spend 10-15 minutes each day visualizing a specific goal. Make it as vivid and detailed as possible, and focus on the emotions you would feel if it were already happening.

3. **Journaling Your Vision**: After each visualization session, write down what you saw and felt in your journal. This helps to reinforce the experience and make it feel more real.

In the next chapter, we'll explore the importance of embracing the unknown and trusting the process, even when things don't go as planned. Visualization is a powerful tool, but it's just one piece of the puzzle. Let's continue this journey together, building the life you've always dreamed of.

Chapter 4: Embracing the Unknown: Trusting the Process

As you embark on your journey to manifest the life you desire, you'll quickly realize that things don't always go according to plan. There will be moments of uncertainty, times when it feels like nothing is happening, and even setbacks that make you question whether you're on the right path. This chapter is all about learning to embrace the unknown and trusting the process, even when the way forward isn't clear.

One of the biggest challenges we face when trying to create something new in our lives is the fear of the unknown. As humans, we naturally crave certainty and control. We want to know exactly how things will unfold and when we'll reach our goals. But the truth is, the journey of manifestation often involves stepping into the unknown, trusting that things will work out even when we can't see the entire path ahead.

When I first started practicing manifestation, I struggled with this a lot. I wanted to know every detail of how my desires would come to fruition. I would create detailed plans and try to control every aspect of the process. But over time, I learned that this approach often led to frustration and disappointment. The more I tried to control everything, the more things seemed to go off course.

Then, I discovered the power of surrender—letting go of the need to control every outcome and trusting that the universe has a plan, even if I couldn't see it. This doesn't mean giving up on your dreams or sitting back and doing nothing. It means taking inspired action while remaining open to different possibilities and trusting that everything is unfolding in perfect timing, even if it doesn't look the way you expected.

One experience that taught me this lesson was when I was working towards a major goal. I had everything planned out, from the steps I needed to take to the timeline I expected to follow. But as I moved forward, things didn't go as planned. Unexpected challenges arose, and my timeline was thrown off track. I started to panic, thinking that my goal was slipping away.

But then, I remembered the importance of trusting the process. I took a step back, reminded myself that the universe often works in mysterious ways, and decided to go with the flow. I continued to take action, but I let go of my need for everything to happen in a specific way. To my surprise, things began to fall into place in ways I hadn't anticipated. New opportunities arose that I hadn't considered, and my goal was achieved—just not in the way I had originally envisioned.

This experience taught me that the universe often has a bigger, better plan for us than we can imagine. But to align with that plan, we need to release our attachment to how things "should" happen and trust that everything is unfolding perfectly, even when it doesn't seem like it.

Here's how you can start embracing the unknown and trusting the process:

1. Let Go of the Need for Control: Recognize that you don't need to have everything figured out right now. Focus on the steps you can take today and trust that the next steps will become clear as you move forward.

2. Stay Open to New Possibilities: Sometimes, the path to your goal might look different from what you expected. Stay open to new ideas, opportunities, and directions that might lead

you to your desired outcome, even if they're not what you initially planned.

3. Practice Patience: Manifestation doesn't always happen on your timeline. Be patient and trust that the universe is working behind the scenes, even when you can't see it. Remember that delays and detours often serve a purpose, guiding you to something even better.

4. Focus on the Present Moment: Instead of worrying about the future or getting stuck in the "how," bring your attention back to the present moment. Ask yourself, "What can I do right now to move closer to my goal?" Taking action in the present helps to keep your energy aligned with your desires.

5. Develop Faith: Faith is the belief in something even when there's no physical evidence to support it. Strengthen your faith by reminding yourself of past experiences where things worked out, even when you couldn't see the way forward.

6. Find Comfort in Uncertainty: Learn to see the unknown as a place of possibility rather than fear. Embrace the fact that anything can happen, and that uncertainty often opens the door to unexpected blessings.

7. Meditation and Mindfulness: Incorporate meditation and mindfulness practices into your routine to help calm your mind and stay centered. These practices can help you connect with your inner guidance and build trust in the process.

Exercises:

1. **Letting Go Ritual**: Write down any fears or anxieties you have about the future on a piece of paper. Then, safely burn the paper (or tear it up) as a symbolic gesture of letting go of control and trusting the process.

2. **Affirmation Practice**: Create an affirmation that resonates with the idea of trust, such as "I trust that everything is unfolding perfectly." Repeat it daily, especially when you feel uncertain or anxious.

3. **Mindfulness Moments**: Throughout your day, practice bringing your attention back to the present moment. Notice the sights, sounds, and sensations around you, and remind yourself that the present is where your power lies.

In the next chapter, we'll delve into the Law of Attraction, a key principle that explains how your thoughts, feelings, and beliefs shape your reality. By understanding this law, you'll learn how to consciously attract the experiences and opportunities you desire. The journey continues, and the magic within you is growing stronger every day.

Chapter 5: The Law of Attraction: What You Focus on Expands

At the heart of manifesting the life you desire is a powerful principle known as the Law of Attraction. This law states that like attracts like—meaning that the energy you put out into the world through your thoughts, feelings, and beliefs comes back to you in the form of experiences and opportunities. In this chapter, we'll explore how the Law of Attraction works and how you can use it to shape your reality.

The Law of Attraction is always at work, whether you're aware of it or not. Every thought you think and every emotion you feel sends out a vibration that attracts similar vibrations back to you. If you're constantly focused on negative thoughts or worries, you'll attract more of those same experiences into your life. On the other hand, when you focus on positive thoughts and emotions, you begin to attract positive experiences and opportunities.

Let me share a story from my own life that illustrates the power of the Law of Attraction. There was a time when I was stuck in a cycle of negativity. I was going through a rough patch, and all I could think about were the things that were going wrong. My thoughts were consumed with worry, frustration, and fear. And sure enough, the more I focused on those negative thoughts, the more things seemed to go wrong. It felt like I was attracting one problem after another.

But then, I learned about the Law of Attraction. I realized that my thoughts and feelings were like a magnet, pulling more of what I was focusing on into my life. So, I decided to experiment. I started by shifting my focus away from what was going wrong and instead began to think about what I wanted to experience. I practiced gratitude, focusing on the things I was thankful for, no matter how small. I began to visualize positive outcomes and imagine how good it would feel to achieve my goals.

At first, it was challenging. My mind kept drifting back to old worries, but I was determined to stick with it. Slowly but surely, I began to notice a change. My mood improved, and I started to feel more optimistic. And then, the most amazing thing happened—my external circumstances began to shift. Opportunities I hadn't expected started to appear, and problems that once seemed overwhelming began to resolve themselves. It was as if the universe was responding to my new, positive energy.

This experience taught me that the Law of Attraction is real and incredibly powerful. What you focus on truly does expand. If you want to attract positive experiences into your life, you need to cultivate positive thoughts and feelings. This doesn't mean ignoring challenges or pretending that everything is perfect. It's about choosing to focus on solutions, possibilities, and the outcomes you desire, rather than dwelling on problems or fears.

Here's how you can start using the Law of Attraction to create the life you want:

1. Become Aware of Your Thoughts: The first step is to become conscious of what you're thinking. Throughout the day, pay attention to your thoughts. Are they mostly positive or negative? Are you focused on what you want or what you don't want? Awareness is the first step to change.

2. Shift Your Focus: If you notice that your thoughts are negative or focused on what you don't want, gently shift your focus to something more positive. For example, if you catch yourself worrying about a problem, shift your focus to thinking about a solution or imagining a positive outcome.

3. Practice Gratitude: Gratitude is one of the most powerful ways to align yourself with positive energy. Each day, take a moment to think about what you're grateful for. It could be something as simple as a beautiful sunset, a kind word from a friend, or even the fact that you're alive and breathing. Gratitude raises your vibration and attracts more things to be grateful for.

4. Use Affirmations: Positive affirmations are a great way to reinforce positive thoughts and beliefs. Create a few affirmations that resonate with you, such as "I am worthy of love and success" or "Good things are always coming to me." Repeat these affirmations daily to help reprogram your mind.

5. Visualize Your Desired Outcome: Spend time each day visualizing what you want to attract into your life. Imagine it as if it's already happening, and focus on the positive feelings it brings. The more vividly you can imagine it, the more powerful your attraction will be.

6. Feel the Emotion: The Law of Attraction isn't just about thinking positively—it's also about feeling positive emotions. The more you can generate feelings of joy, love, excitement, and gratitude, the more you'll attract those experiences into your life.

7. Take Inspired Action: While the Law of Attraction is powerful, it works best when combined with action. Pay attention to any intuitive nudges or ideas that come to you after focusing on what you want. These are often signs from the universe guiding you towards your goals. Act on them!

As you begin to apply the Law of Attraction in your life, remember that it's a practice. It takes time to shift your mindset and energy, especially if you've been focused on the negative for a long time. Be patient with yourself and trust the process. The more you focus on what you want and cultivate positive energy, the more you'll begin to see changes in your life.

Exercises:

1. **Thought Awareness Journal:** Start a journal where you write down your thoughts throughout the day. Note whether they're positive or negative and how they make you feel. Over time, you'll start to see patterns and areas where you can shift your focus.

2. **Gratitude List:** Every day, write down three things you're grateful for. Try to choose different things each day to keep your focus on the many blessings in your life.

3. **Affirmation Practice:** Choose one or two affirmations that resonate with you and repeat them every morning and night. You can also write them down and place them somewhere you'll see them often, like on your mirror or desk.

In the next chapter, we'll explore how to overcome the obstacles and limiting beliefs that might be blocking you from fully embracing the Law of Attraction. Remember, what you focus on expands—so let's focus on creating the life of your dreams! The journey continues, and with each step, you're getting closer to manifesting your desires.

Chapter 6: Overcoming Obstacles and Limiting Beliefs

As you continue your journey with the Law of Attraction and the practice of manifesting your desires, you may encounter obstacles that seem to block your progress. These obstacles often come in the form of limiting beliefs—deep-seated thoughts or assumptions that tell you what you can or cannot achieve. In this chapter, we'll explore how to identify and overcome these limiting beliefs so that you can fully embrace your power to create the life you want.

Limiting beliefs are like invisible chains that hold you back from reaching your full potential. They often develop in childhood, based on experiences, observations, or things we've been told by others. For example, if you were told as a child that "money doesn't grow on trees," you might have developed a belief that wealth is hard to come by. Or if you were criticized for making mistakes, you might believe that you're not capable of success.

The tricky thing about limiting beliefs is that they often operate unconsciously. You may not even be aware that you have them, but they still influence your thoughts, feelings, and actions. These beliefs can create self-doubt, fear, and resistance, which in turn prevent you from fully embracing the Law of Attraction and manifesting your desires.

One of the most powerful lessons I've learned on my own journey is that the only limits that truly exist are the ones we place on ourselves. When I first started working with the Law of Attraction, I had to confront many of my own limiting beliefs.

For example, I used to believe that success was something that only came to certain people—those who were born into the right circumstances or who had special talents. This belief held me back from pursuing my dreams because I didn't see myself as one of those "lucky" people.

But then I learned that these beliefs were just stories I had been telling myself, and they weren't true. I realized that I had the power to rewrite those stories and create new, empowering beliefs that would support my goals. It wasn't easy—it required a lot of introspection and effort—but the results were life-changing.

Here's how you can begin to identify and overcome your own limiting beliefs:

1. Identify Your Limiting Beliefs: The first step is to become aware of the beliefs that are holding you back. Start by paying attention to the thoughts that come up when you think about your goals. Do you hear an inner voice saying things like "I'm not good enough," "I don't deserve this," or "It's too hard"? These thoughts are clues to your limiting beliefs.

2. Challenge Your Beliefs: Once you've identified a limiting belief, ask yourself if it's really true. Is there evidence to support it, or is it just a story you've been telling yourself? For example, if you believe that "I'm not good enough," ask yourself, "What does 'good enough' really mean, and who gets to decide that?" You may find that these beliefs are based on assumptions rather than facts.

3. Replace Limiting Beliefs with Empowering Ones: After challenging your limiting beliefs, it's time to replace them with new, empowering beliefs. For example, if your limiting belief is "I'm not good enough," you might replace it with "I am capable,

and I deserve to succeed." Write down your new beliefs and repeat them to yourself regularly. The more you affirm these new beliefs, the more they will become your reality.

4. Take Action Despite Your Beliefs: Sometimes, the best way to overcome a limiting belief is to take action in spite of it. If you believe that you're not capable of achieving a goal, take a small step towards it anyway. Each time you take action, you'll begin to build evidence that contradicts your old belief, which will help you to let it go.

5. Surround Yourself with Positive Influences: The people you spend time with and the environment you're in can have a big impact on your beliefs. Surround yourself with people who support and encourage your dreams. Seek out books, podcasts, and other resources that inspire you and reinforce your new, empowering beliefs.

6. Practice Self-Compassion: Changing your beliefs takes time and effort, and it's normal to encounter setbacks along the way. Be kind to yourself and recognize that you're on a journey of growth. Celebrate your progress, no matter how small, and keep moving forward.

7. Visualize Your Empowered Self: Spend time each day visualizing yourself living according to your new, empowering beliefs. Imagine what it would feel like to fully embrace your power and achieve your goals. The more you can see and feel this in your mind, the more it will become your reality.

As you begin to identify and release your limiting beliefs, you'll notice that the obstacles that once seemed insurmountable start to disappear. You'll feel more confident, more empowered, and more aligned with your true potential. Remember, the only limits that exist are the ones you place on yourself—and you have the power to remove them.

Exercises:

1. **Belief Inventory:** Take some time to write down all the beliefs you have about yourself, your abilities, and your goals. Which ones are empowering, and which ones are limiting? Circle the limiting beliefs and challenge them by asking, "Is this really true?"

2. **Affirmation Creation:** Based on the limiting beliefs you've identified, create new affirmations that reflect the empowering beliefs you want to adopt. Write them down and repeat them daily, especially when you notice your old beliefs creeping back in.

3. **Action Challenge:** Choose one small action that challenges a limiting belief you have. For example, if you believe that you're not good at speaking in public, volunteer to give a short presentation. Taking action will help you build confidence and prove to yourself that your old belief isn't true.

In the next chapter, we'll explore the role of energy and vibration in the manifestation process. You'll learn how to raise your vibration and align your energy with your desires, making it easier for you to attract the life you want. The journey continues, and with each chapter, you're becoming more powerful and more aligned with the magic within you.

Chapter 7: The Power of Vibration: Aligning Your Energy with Your Desires

In the world of manifestation, everything is made up of energy, and this energy vibrates at different frequencies. The Law of Attraction, which we discussed earlier, operates on the principle that like attracts like—meaning that the vibration you emit attracts experiences, people, and circumstances that match that frequency. In this chapter, we'll dive into the concept of vibration and explore how you can raise your energy to align with your desires, making it easier to manifest the life you want.

To understand vibration, imagine that your thoughts, emotions, and beliefs are like a radio signal. When you tune into a specific frequency, you receive the broadcast that matches it. Similarly, when you focus on certain thoughts or feelings, you're sending out a signal that attracts corresponding experiences into your life. If your energy is low—filled with fear, doubt, or negativity—you're likely to attract experiences that match that low vibration. But when your energy is high—filled with love, joy, and positivity—you attract more of the same.

I first became aware of the importance of vibration when I noticed that certain days felt effortless and full of synchronicities, while others were full of challenges and setbacks. On the good days, I felt light, happy, and in the flow of life. On the tough days, I felt heavy, stressed, and out of sync. I began to realize that these different experiences were directly linked to my state of mind and emotions—the higher my vibration, the better my day went.

One of the most profound lessons I learned is that you have the power to change your vibration at any moment. By consciously choosing thoughts, feelings, and actions that raise your energy, you can shift your vibration and attract more positive experiences into your life. This doesn't mean you'll never face challenges, but it does mean that you'll be better equipped to handle them and bounce back more quickly.

Here's how you can start raising your vibration and aligning your energy with your desires:

1. Practice Gratitude: Gratitude is one of the quickest ways to raise your vibration. When you focus on what you're thankful for, you shift your energy from a state of lack to a state of abundance. Take a few moments each day to think about or write down what you're grateful for. As you do, notice how your energy lifts.

2. Choose Joy: Joy is a high-vibration emotion that attracts more joy into your life. Look for ways to bring more joy into your day, whether it's spending time with loved ones, engaging in a hobby, or simply doing something that makes you laugh. The more you focus on joy, the more joyful experiences you'll attract.

3. Surround Yourself with Positivity: The people, environments, and media you consume all influence your vibration. Surround yourself with positive influences that uplift and inspire you. Spend time with people who support your dreams, and limit exposure to negativity, whether it's in the news, social media, or toxic relationships.

4. Practice Mindfulness: Mindfulness helps you stay present and connected to your inner self, which naturally raises your vibration. Whether through meditation, deep breathing, or simply being aware of your thoughts and feelings, mindfulness

allows you to tune into your energy and make conscious choices about how you respond to life's challenges.

5. Visualize Your Desires: Visualization is a powerful tool for aligning your energy with your goals. Spend time each day visualizing what you want to manifest. Imagine it in as much detail as possible, and focus on the positive emotions it brings. This not only raises your vibration but also strengthens your belief in the possibility of your desires coming true.

6. Let Go of Low-Vibration Emotions: Emotions like fear, anger, and resentment can lower your vibration and block the flow of positive energy. When these emotions arise, acknowledge them without judgment, and then consciously choose to release them. Techniques like journaling, talking to a friend, or simply taking deep breaths can help you let go and return to a higher state of being.

7. Take Care of Your Physical Body: Your physical health is closely connected to your energy levels. Eating nourishing foods, staying hydrated, getting enough sleep, and exercising regularly all contribute to raising your vibration. Treat your body with care, and it will reward you with higher energy and a greater sense of well-being.

8. Set Positive Intentions: Each morning, set an intention for how you want to feel and what you want to attract that day. For example, you might say, "Today, I choose to feel peaceful and attract positive experiences." By setting an intention, you align your energy with your desired outcomes and create a roadmap for your day.

Exercises:

1. **Vibration Check-In:** Throughout the day, pause and check in with yourself. How are you feeling? What thoughts are

running through your mind? If you notice your vibration is low, take a few deep breaths, and choose a thought or action that raises your energy.

2. **Gratitude Journal:** Keep a daily gratitude journal where you write down at least three things you're grateful for each day. Reflect on how practicing gratitude shifts your mood and energy over time.

3. **Positive Affirmations:** Create a list of positive affirmations that resonate with you, such as "I am full of positive energy" or "I attract abundance into my life." Repeat these affirmations daily to help raise your vibration and align with your desires.

In the next chapter, we'll explore the concept of inspired action—how to recognize and act on the intuitive nudges and opportunities that guide you towards your goals. Remember, your vibration is the key to unlocking the life you want. As you raise your energy and align with your desires, you'll find that the universe responds in kind, bringing you closer to the life of your dreams. The journey continues, and with each step, your inner magic shines brighter and brighter.

Chapter 8: Inspired Action: Following the Signs from the Universe

As you continue to align your vibration with your desires, you'll start to notice that the universe seems to respond in surprising and wonderful ways. Opportunities, ideas, and even people may appear seemingly out of nowhere, guiding you closer to your goals. This is the magic of inspired action—when you feel a strong, intuitive nudge to take a specific action that aligns perfectly with what you're trying to manifest. In this chapter, we'll explore what inspired action is, how to recognize it, and why it's a crucial part of the manifestation process.

What Is Inspired Action?

Inspired action is different from the regular, everyday actions you might take to achieve a goal. It's not something you force or plan out meticulously. Instead, it feels like a natural, almost effortless next step. It's the kind of action that feels exciting, aligned, and filled with possibility. When you're in tune with your desires and your vibration is high, inspired action flows easily and leads to the outcomes you want, often in ways you couldn't have predicted.

For example, let's say you've been visualizing and focusing on manifesting a new job that aligns with your passions. One day, while casually browsing the internet, you come across an article that mentions a company you've never heard of before. You feel a sudden, strong urge to check out their website, and as you do, you discover that they're hiring for a position that seems perfect for you. This is a moment of inspired action—an intuitive nudge from the universe guiding you toward what you want.

How to Recognize Inspired Action

Recognizing inspired action can sometimes be tricky because it often comes in subtle, unexpected ways.

Here are some signs to help you identify when you're being guided to take inspired action:

1. It Feels Exciting and Aligned: Inspired action often feels exciting and deeply aligned with your goals. You might feel a sense of enthusiasm, curiosity, or a strong "yes" feeling when the idea or opportunity presents itself.

2. It Comes Unexpectedly: Inspired ideas often come out of the blue. You might be doing something unrelated, like taking a walk or relaxing, when suddenly an idea or urge pops into your mind. These moments of inspiration are often clues from the universe.

3. It Feels Effortless: Unlike forced actions that require a lot of planning or struggle, inspired action feels easy and natural. It's as if everything just falls into place, and the next step is clear.

4. You Feel a Strong Inner Knowing: Sometimes, inspired action comes with a deep, inner knowing that this is the right thing to do. You may not be able to explain why, but you just know that this is the path you should take.

5. It Brings Synchronicities: When you follow inspired action, you might notice that synchronicities—meaningful coincidences—start to occur. These are signs that you're on the right track and that the universe is supporting your journey.

Why Inspired Action Is Important

Inspired action is a key part of the manifestation process because it bridges the gap between your desires and reality.

While visualizing and raising your vibration are essential, they must be coupled with action to bring your dreams to life. Inspired action is like a green light from the universe, signaling that it's time to move forward and that the path is clear.

Taking inspired action also shows the universe that you're serious about your desires. It's a way of saying, "I'm ready, and I trust that this is the right step." When you take action, even small steps, you create momentum and open yourself up to more opportunities and guidance.

How to Cultivate Inspired Action

To cultivate inspired action, you need to stay in tune with your intuition and remain open to the signs and nudges from the universe. Here's how you can do that:

1. Stay Present and Mindful: Inspired action often arises when you're present and connected to the moment. Practice mindfulness and stay aware of your thoughts, feelings, and the world around you. This will help you notice when inspiration strikes.

2. Trust Your Intuition: Your intuition is your inner guidance system, and it's often the source of inspired ideas. Trust the feelings and urges that arise from within, even if they don't always make logical sense. Remember, inspired action often comes from a deeper knowing rather than from logical reasoning.

3. Let Go of Over thinking: Sometimes, over thinking can block inspired action. If you find yourself analyzing every detail or doubting your instincts, take a step back. Relax, and allow yourself to trust that the universe is guiding you. The more you let go of the need to control everything, the easier it will be to recognize and act on inspiration.

4. Act Quickly: When inspiration strikes, act on it as soon as possible. The more you delay, the more doubt and resistance can creep in. By taking quick action, you keep the energy flowing and build momentum toward your goals.

5. Stay Open to Possibilities: Inspired action may not always look the way you expect. Stay open to new ideas, opportunities, and paths that may present themselves. Sometimes, the universe has a better plan than the one you had in mind.

Exercises:

1. **Daily Inspiration Journal:** Keep a journal where you write down any inspired ideas, urges, or synchronicities that occur throughout the day. Reflect on these moments and notice how they guide you toward your desires.

2. **Intuitive Decision-Making:** Practice making decisions based on your intuition rather than over thinking. Start with small decisions, like what to eat or which route to take, and notice how it feels to trust your inner guidance.

3. **Take an Inspired Step:** Think of a goal you're currently working on. What's one inspired action you can take today to move closer to that goal? It doesn't have to be big—sometimes, the smallest steps lead to the most significant results.

—-

In the next chapter, we'll explore the role of faith and surrender in the manifestation process. You'll learn how to let go of attachment to outcomes and trust that the universe is working behind the scenes to bring your desires to fruition. The journey of manifestation is one of co-creation, and with each chapter, you're deepening your understanding of the magic that lies within you. Keep moving forward with faith and inspired action, and watch as your dreams unfold in ways you never imagined.

Chapter 9: The Art of Surrender: Letting Go and Trusting the Process

As you journey through the world of manifestation, you'll discover that one of the most powerful practices is learning to surrender. Surrender doesn't mean giving up on your dreams; rather, it's about letting go of the need to control every detail and trusting that the universe has your back. In this chapter, we'll explore the art of surrender, why it's essential for manifesting your desires, and how you can cultivate a mindset of trust and faith in the process.

What Does Surrender Mean in Manifestation?

In the context of manifestation, surrender means releasing your attachment to how and when your desires will come to fruition. It's about trusting that the universe is orchestrating things in the best possible way, even if you can't see the whole picture yet. When you surrender, you're saying, "I trust that everything is unfolding perfectly, and I'm open to receiving what is meant for me in divine timing."

I remember when I first began practicing surrender, it was challenging. I was used to planning everything and trying to make things happen according to my timeline. But as I delved deeper into the practice of manifestation, I realized that the more I tried to control the outcome, the more resistance I created. It was only when I learned to let go and trust the process that things started to flow more effortlessly.

Why Surrender Is Important

Surrender is a crucial part of manifestation because it allows you to release resistance and align with the flow of the universe.

When you're attached to a specific outcome or timeline, you can unknowingly create blocks that prevent your desires from manifesting. This attachment often stems from fear or doubt—fear that things won't work out or doubt that you're deserving of what you want. By surrendering, you release these lower vibrations and open yourself up to the infinite possibilities that the universe has in store.

Surrender also brings a sense of peace and ease to the manifestation process. Instead of stressing about how everything will come together, you can relax and enjoy the journey. This shift in mindset not only makes the process more enjoyable but also raises your vibration, making it easier for your desires to manifest.

How to Practice Surrender

Surrendering is a practice that requires trust, patience, and faith. Here are some ways to cultivate the art of surrender in your life:

1. Set Your Intentions, Then Let Go: Start by setting clear intentions for what you want to manifest. Visualize your desires, feel the emotions associated with them, and take inspired action. But after you've done this, let go of the need to control how it will happen. Trust that the universe knows the best way to bring your desires to you.

2. Embrace Uncertainty: Uncertainty is a natural part of life, and it's also a key element of surrender. Instead of fearing the unknown, embrace it as an opportunity for growth and discovery. Trust that even when things seem uncertain, the universe is guiding you toward what's best for you.

3. Release Attachment to Outcomes: One of the biggest challenges in surrendering is releasing attachment to specific

outcomes. Practice focusing on the feelings and experiences you want to attract rather than the exact form they should take. For example, if you're manifesting a new job, focus on the feelings of fulfillment, joy, and abundance, rather than fixating on a particular job title or company.

4. Trust in Divine Timing: Sometimes, your desires take longer to manifest than you'd like. This doesn't mean they won't happen; it simply means that the timing isn't right yet. Trust that everything is unfolding in perfect timing, and be patient with the process.

5. Practice Mindfulness and Presence: Surrendering often requires staying present in the moment and letting go of worries about the future. Practice mindfulness by bringing your awareness to the present moment and focusing on what you can do right now to align with your desires. The more present you are, the easier it is to trust the process.

6. Affirm Your Trust: Use affirmations to reinforce your trust in the universe. Statements like "I trust that everything is working out for my highest good" or "I surrender and allow the universe to guide me" can help you cultivate a mindset of trust and faith.

How to Know When You've Truly Surrendered

Surrendering is not a one-time event but a continuous practice. You'll know you've truly surrendered when you feel a sense of peace and acceptance, regardless of what's happening around you. You're no longer anxious about the outcome, and you trust that everything is unfolding perfectly, even if it doesn't look that way right now. When you've surrendered, you're able to enjoy the journey, appreciate the present moment, and remain open to the unexpected gifts and opportunities that come your way.

Exercises:

1. **Surrender Meditation:** Practice a surrender meditation where you visualize your desires and then imagine placing them in the hands of the universe. As you do, repeat a mantra like "I release control and trust the universe" or "I surrender my desires to the divine timing and wisdom of the universe."

2. **Release Ritual:** Write down any fears, doubts, or attachments you have regarding your desires. Then, perform a release ritual by either burning the paper (safely) or tearing it up and throwing it away. As you do, affirm your trust in the universe and your willingness to let go.

3. **Daily Surrender Practice:** Each morning, take a few moments to set your intentions for the day and then consciously surrender them to the universe. Say something like, "I trust that today will unfold perfectly, and I'm open to whatever comes my way."

In the next chapter, we'll explore the concept of faith—how to cultivate unwavering belief in your ability to manifest your desires and how to maintain that faith even in the face of challenges. Remember, surrender is not about giving up; it's about trusting that the universe is working behind the scenes to bring you everything you've asked for. As you practice surrender, you'll find that life becomes more magical, filled with synchronicities, and guided by a sense of ease and flow. Keep trusting, keep surrendering, and watch as the universe works its magic in your life.

Chapter 10: Cultivating Unwavering Faith: Believing in Your Manifestation Journey

Faith is the cornerstone of the manifestation process. It's the unshakeable belief that what you desire is already on its way to you, even if you can't see it yet. In this chapter, we'll delve into the concept of faith, why it's essential for manifesting your dreams, and how you can cultivate and maintain unwavering belief in your ability to bring your desires to fruition.

What Is Faith in Manifestation?

In the context of manifestation, faith is about having complete confidence in the process and trusting that your desires are being fulfilled, even if you don't have immediate evidence of it. It's the inner certainty that your goals are on their way, and you are deserving of receiving them. This faith acts as a powerful magnet, drawing your desires closer to you by maintaining a positive and hopeful outlook.

For instance, when I first started practicing manifestation, there were times when it felt like nothing was happening. Despite my efforts, I saw no visible signs of progress. It was during these moments that my faith was tested. However, by reminding myself of the principles of manifestation and trusting in the process, I was able to maintain my belief. Eventually, I started to see the fruits of my efforts manifest in ways I couldn't have anticipated.

Why Faith Is Crucial

Faith is crucial because it fuels your persistence and resilience. When you have unwavering belief in your goals, you are more likely to stay motivated and take the necessary actions, even when faced with obstacles. Faith also helps you maintain a positive mindset, which is essential for keeping your vibration high and aligned with your desires.

Without faith, doubt and fear can creep in, creating resistance and blocking the flow of manifestation. Faith helps you overcome these negative emotions and stay focused on what you want to achieve. It acts as a bridge between your current reality and the reality you are creating, helping you navigate the journey with confidence and grace.

How to Cultivate Unwavering Faith

Cultivating faith requires practice and a shift in mindset. Here's how you can build and strengthen your belief in your manifestation journey:

1. *Visualize Your Success*: Visualization is a powerful tool for reinforcing your faith. Spend time each day imagining your desires as if they've already been fulfilled. Feel the emotions associated with achieving your goals and see the details of your success. This practice helps you create a mental image of what's possible, making it easier to believe in its reality.

2. *Affirm Your Beliefs:* Use positive affirmations to strengthen your faith. Statements like "I have unwavering faith in my ability to manifest my desires" or "Everything I want is on its way to me" can help reinforce your belief and keep you focused on your goals.

3. *Remind Yourself of Past Successes*: Reflect on times in your life when you've achieved something you once thought was impossible. Reminding yourself of past successes can boost your confidence and reinforce your faith in the manifestation process.

4. *Surround Yourself with Positivity:* The people you interact with and the environments you're in can influence your faith. Surround yourself with supportive, positive individuals who encourage your dreams and believe in your potential. Avoid negativity and skepticism that can undermine your faith.

5. *Practice Gratitude:* Gratitude is a powerful tool for maintaining faith. By focusing on what you already have and appreciating the progress you've made, you reinforce a positive mindset and strengthen your belief that more good is on its way.

6. *Trust in Divine Timing:* Understand that the universe has its own timing for delivering your desires. Trust that everything is unfolding in perfect timing, even if it doesn't happen as quickly as you'd like. Patience and trust in divine timing help you maintain faith and stay aligned with your goals.

7. *Stay Consistent:* Consistency is key to maintaining faith. Regularly engage in practices that support your manifestation journey, such as visualization, affirmations, and positive actions. Consistency helps you stay focused and reinforces your belief in your ability to achieve your goals.

8. *Seek Inspiration:* Read books, watch videos, or listen to podcasts that inspire and motivate you. Learning from others who have successfully manifested their desires can boost your faith and provide valuable insights into the process.

How to Maintain Faith Through Challenges

Challenges and setbacks are a natural part of any journey. When faced with obstacles, it's important to maintain your faith and stay committed to your goals. Here's how to navigate challenges while keeping your faith intact:

1. Reframe Setbacks as Opportunities: View challenges as opportunities for growth and learning. Instead of seeing setbacks

as failures, consider them as valuable lessons that help you become more resilient and prepared for future success.

2. Focus on the Bigger Picture: When you encounter difficulties, remind yourself of the bigger picture and your long-term goals. This perspective helps you stay focused on what you want to achieve and reinforces your faith in the process.

3. Practice Self-Care: Taking care of yourself physically, emotionally, and mentally helps you stay strong and maintain faith. Engage in activities that nurture your well-being and help you stay positive during challenging times.

4. Seek Support: Reach out to supportive friends, mentors, or coaches who can offer encouragement and guidance. Having a support system can help you stay motivated and maintain your faith, even when facing obstacles.

Exercises:

1. **Faith Journal:** Keep a journal where you write about your goals, dreams, and the faith you have in achieving them. Reflect on any challenges you face and how you can maintain faith in the process. Review your entries regularly to reinforce your belief and track your progress.

2. **Affirmation Practice**: Create a list of affirmations that strengthen your faith and belief in your manifestation journey. Repeat these affirmations daily, especially during moments of doubt or uncertainty.

3. **Success Reflection:** Make a list of past successes and accomplishments, no matter how small. Reflect on how these achievements were once dreams that you believed in and how they became a reality. Use this reflection to boost your faith in your current goals.

In the next chapter, we'll explore the role of persistence in manifestation—the importance of staying committed to your goals and continuing to take inspired action, even when progress seems slow. With unwavering faith as your foundation, you'll find that persistence becomes a natural extension of your journey. Keep believing, keep taking action, and watch as your dreams unfold before you. The path to manifestation is illuminated by faith and persistence, and with each step, you're drawing closer to the life you envision.

Chapter 11: The Power of Persistence: *Staying Committed to Your Goals*

Persistence is a key element of successful manifestation. It's the determination to continue working towards your goals, even when progress seems slow or obstacles arise. In this chapter, we'll explore why persistence is so important in the manifestation process, how to cultivate it, and strategies to stay committed to your dreams even in the face of challenges.

What Is Persistence in Manifestation?

Persistence in manifestation is about maintaining your commitment and effort towards your goals, despite any setbacks or delays. It's the unwavering drive to keep moving forward and taking action, even when results are not immediately visible. Persistence involves a combination of patience, resilience, and consistent effort, all of which play a crucial role in bringing your desires to fruition.

For example, when I was working on manifesting a significant career shift, there were times when it felt like nothing was happening. I faced rejections and delays, but my commitment to my goal never wavered. By staying persistent and continuing to take inspired actions, I eventually saw progress and achieved the career change I had been working towards.

Why Persistence Is Crucial

Persistence is crucial because it helps you overcome the inevitable challenges and obstacles that arise on the path to achieving your goals. Without persistence, it's easy to give up at the first sign of difficulty or to become discouraged when things don't go as planned. Persistence ensures that you keep moving forward, even when the journey is tough, and helps you stay focused on the end result.

Moreover, persistence reinforces your belief in your ability to manifest your desires. Each step you take, no matter how small, brings you closer to your goal and strengthens your confidence. It also creates momentum, making it easier to attract more opportunities and resources as you continue to work towards your dreams.

How to Cultivate Persistence

Cultivating persistence involves developing a mindset and habits that support your commitment to your goals. Here's how you can build and maintain persistence:

1. Set Clear and Specific Goals: Having clear, specific goals gives you direction and purpose. When you know exactly what you want to achieve, it's easier to stay focused and motivated, even when faced with challenges.

2. Break Goals into Smaller Steps: Large goals can sometimes feel overwhelming. Break them down into smaller, manageable steps and focus on completing one step at a time. This approach makes the process more manageable and helps you stay committed.

3. Create a Plan of Action: Develop a plan outlining the steps you need to take to achieve your goals. Having a plan provides structure and helps you stay organized, making it easier to maintain persistence.

4. Stay Flexible and Adaptable: While persistence is important, it's also essential to remain flexible and adaptable. Be

open to adjusting your plan or approach if needed. Flexibility allows you to navigate obstacles and find alternative solutions without losing sight of your goal.

5. Develop a Positive Mindset: Cultivate a positive mindset by focusing on your progress and celebrating small victories. Positive thinking helps you stay motivated and reinforces your commitment to your goals.

6. Build a Support System: Surround yourself with supportive friends, family, or mentors who encourage and inspire you. A strong support system can provide motivation and help you stay persistent, especially during challenging times.

7. Practice Self-Discipline: Develop self-discipline by creating and sticking to daily or weekly routines that support your goals. Consistent effort and habits contribute to your persistence and overall success.

8. Visualize Your Success: Regularly visualize yourself achieving your goals and experiencing the success you desire. Visualization reinforces your commitment and helps you stay focused on the end result.

9. Stay Resilient in the Face of Setbacks: Understand that setbacks are a natural part of the journey. When you encounter obstacles, use them as opportunities to learn and grow. Resilience helps you bounce back and continue moving forward.

Strategies for Maintaining Persistence

Maintaining persistence can be challenging, especially when progress is slow or obstacles arise. Here are some strategies to help you stay committed to your goals:

1. Track Your Progress: Keep a journal or record of your progress towards your goals. Regularly reviewing your

achievements and milestones can boost your motivation and remind you of how far you've come.

2. Set Short-Term Milestones: Establish short-term milestones that lead up to your long-term goals. Achieving these smaller milestones provides a sense of accomplishment and keeps you motivated to continue.

3. Stay Accountable: Share your goals with a trusted friend or mentor who can hold you accountable and offer support. Regular check-ins and accountability can help you stay focused and persistent.

4. Revisit Your "Why": Remind yourself of the reasons why you set your goals in the first place. Connecting with your "why" provides motivation and helps you stay committed, even when faced with challenges.

5. Practice Patience: Understand that manifestation takes time and effort. Practice patience and trust the process, knowing that your persistence is building momentum and bringing you closer to your desires.

Exercises:

1. **Persistence Tracker:** Create a tracker or journal to monitor your progress towards your goals. Record your actions, milestones, and any challenges you face. Reflect on your achievements and areas for improvement regularly.

2. **Action Plan:** Develop a detailed action plan for achieving your goals, including specific steps, deadlines, and resources needed. Review and update your plan as needed to stay on track and maintain persistence.

3. **Resilience Reflection:** Reflect on past challenges you've overcome and how persistence played a role in your success. Use

these reflections as reminders of your ability to stay committed and achieve your goals.

In the next chapter, we'll explore the importance of self-care and balance in the manifestation process. As you persist in working towards your goals, it's essential to take care of yourself and maintain a balanced approach. By integrating self-care practices into your journey, you'll enhance your overall well-being and create a harmonious environment for your desires to manifest. Keep moving forward with determination and self-compassion, and watch as your dreams become reality.

Chapter 12: Embracing Self-Care and Balance: *Nurturing Yourself on the Manifestation Journey*

Self-care and balance are vital components of a successful manifestation journey. While persistence and action are crucial, it's equally important to take care of yourself and maintain equilibrium in your life. In this chapter, we'll explore the role of self-care and balance in manifestation, how to incorporate them into your routine, and why they are essential for achieving your goals and maintaining overall well-being.

What Is Self-Care in Manifestation?

Self-care involves taking intentional actions to nurture your physical, emotional, mental, and spiritual well-being. It's about prioritizing your needs and ensuring that you're in a healthy and balanced state to support your manifestation efforts. Self-care is not just about pampering yourself; it's about creating a sustainable foundation for your personal growth and success.

During my own manifestation journey, I learned that neglecting self-care led to burnout and diminished motivation. By incorporating self-care practices into my routine, I found that I was more focused, energized, and better able to handle the ups and downs of the process. Self-care became an integral part of my journey, enhancing my overall experience and contributing to my success.

Why Self-Care and Balance Are Important

Self-care and balance are important for several reasons:

1. Preventing Burnout: Manifesting your goals requires effort and dedication, but without proper self-care, it's easy to become overwhelmed and exhausted. Regular self-care helps you recharge and prevent burnout, ensuring that you can continue working towards your goals with sustained energy.

2. Maintaining Motivation: Taking care of yourself keeps your motivation levels high. When you're physically and emotionally well, you're more likely to stay focused and enthusiastic about your goals.

3. Enhancing Clarity and Focus: Self-care practices, such as meditation and relaxation, help clear your mind and enhance your focus. This clarity allows you to make better decisions and stay aligned with your goals.

4. Balancing Energy: Manifestation involves both action and receptivity. Balancing your energy through self-care ensures that you're not solely focused on doing but also on receiving and enjoying the process.

5. Cultivating Positive Emotions: Self-care helps you cultivate positive emotions and maintain a high vibration. When you're in a good emotional state, you attract more positive experiences and opportunities.

How to Incorporate Self-Care and Balance

Incorporating self-care and balance into your routine involves creating habits and practices that support your overall well-being. Here's how you can do it:

1. Prioritize Your Well-Being: Make self-care a priority by scheduling regular time for activities that nurture you. This could include exercise, relaxation, hobbies, or spending time with loved ones.

2. Practice Mindfulness and Relaxation: Engage in mindfulness practices such as meditation, deep breathing, or yoga to reduce stress and promote relaxation. These practices help you stay centered and focused on your goals.

3. Establish Healthy Boundaries: Set boundaries to protect your time and energy. Avoid over committing yourself and learn to say no when necessary. Creating space for rest and rejuvenation is essential for maintaining balance.

4. Nurture Your Physical Health: Take care of your body by eating nutritious foods, staying hydrated, and getting regular exercise. Physical health directly impacts your energy levels and overall well-being.

5. Engage in Activities You Enjoy: Make time for activities that bring you joy and fulfillment. Pursuing your passions and interests helps you maintain a positive mindset and prevents burnout.

6. Connect with Others: Build and maintain supportive relationships with friends, family, or mentors. Social connections provide emotional support and help you stay motivated and balanced.

7. Practice Self-Compassion: Be kind and compassionate towards yourself. Acknowledge your efforts and achievements, and avoid self-criticism. Self-compassion helps you stay positive and resilient.

8. Create a Balanced Routine: Develop a daily or weekly routine that includes a mix of work, self-care, and leisure activities. Balance ensures that you're not solely focused on achieving your goals but also on enjoying the journey.

9.*Reflect and Adjust: Regularly reflect on your self-care practices and overall balance. Make adjustments as needed to ensure that you're maintaining a healthy and sustainable approach to your manifestation journey.

Exercises:

1. **Self-Care Checklist**: Create a checklist of self-care activities that you enjoy and find rejuvenating. Schedule time for these activities throughout your week and track your progress.

2. **Mindfulness Practice:** Set aside a few minutes each day for mindfulness or meditation. Use this time to focus on your breath, release stress, and connect with your inner self.

3. **Balance Assessment:** Assess your current balance between work, self-care, and leisure. Identify any areas where you may be out of balance and make adjustments to create a more harmonious routine.

4. **Gratitude Journal:** Keep a gratitude journal where you record things you're grateful for each day. Practicing gratitude helps you stay positive and appreciate the present moment.

In the next chapter, we'll explore the power of manifestation in action—how to turn your dreams into reality through inspired action and practical steps. As you continue to care for yourself and maintain balance, you'll be ready to take the steps needed to bring your desires to life. Embrace self-care as a vital part of your manifestation journey, and let it support you as you move closer to achieving your dreams. With a balanced and nurturing approach, you'll create the space for your desires to manifest and thrive.

Chapter 13: Manifestation in Action: Turning Dreams into Reality

Now that you've built a foundation of self-care, balance, and persistence, it's time to put your dreams into action. Manifestation is not just about visualizing and believing; it's also about taking inspired and practical steps to bring your desires to life. In this chapter, we'll explore how to turn your dreams into reality through actionable strategies, goal setting, and proactive steps.

What Is Manifestation in Action?

Manifestation in action involves translating your dreams and desires into tangible results by taking deliberate and inspired steps. It's about moving beyond thoughts and feelings to actively create the conditions needed for your goals to materialize. This process requires a combination of strategic planning, effective execution, and maintaining a positive mindset.

When I started manifesting my goal of launching a successful business, I realized that simply visualizing success wasn't enough. I had to take concrete steps, like developing a business plan, networking with potential clients, and continuously improving my skills. By aligning my actions with my vision, I was able to bring my dream to fruition.

Why Action Is Essential

Action is essential because it bridges the gap between your desires and reality. While belief and visualization set the stage, action is the means through which you create tangible results. Taking action moves you from a state of wishing and hoping to actively working towards your goals.

Without action, even the strongest belief and visualization can remain just dreams. Action provides momentum, creates opportunities, and demonstrates your commitment to achieving your goals. It also helps you overcome procrastination and take ownership of your manifestation journey.

How to Take Inspired and Practical Action

Taking inspired and practical action involves aligning your efforts with your goals while remaining open to guidance and opportunities. Here's how to effectively turn your dreams into reality:

1. Set Specific Goals: Define clear, specific goals that align with your vision. Break them down into smaller, actionable steps to make them more manageable. For example, if your goal is to write a book, your smaller steps might include outlining the chapters, writing a certain number of words each day, and editing the drafts.

2. Create an Action Plan: Develop a detailed action plan outlining the steps you need to take to achieve your goals. Include deadlines, resources needed, and milestones to track your progress. An action plan provides structure and helps you stay organized.

3. Take Small Steps Daily: Break your goals into daily or weekly tasks and consistently work on them. Small, consistent actions build momentum and keep you on track towards your larger goal.

4. Be Open to Inspiration: While planning is important, stay open to inspiration and opportunities that may arise unexpectedly. Sometimes, the universe presents new paths and ideas that can enhance your manifestation journey.

5. Seek Feedback and Learn: Actively seek feedback from mentors, peers, or experts in your field. Use this feedback to refine your approach and improve your strategies. Learning from others helps you grow and adapt.

6. Stay Flexible: Be prepared to adjust your plans and actions as needed. Flexibility allows you to navigate obstacles and seize new opportunities that align with your goals.

7. Monitor Your Progress: Regularly review your progress and make any necessary adjustments to your action plan. Tracking your progress helps you stay motivated and ensures that you're moving in the right direction.

8. Celebrate Milestones: Celebrate your achievements and milestones along the way. Recognizing and celebrating your progress keeps you motivated and reinforces your commitment to your goals.

9. Maintain a Positive Attitude: Stay positive and focused, even when facing challenges or setbacks. A positive attitude helps you overcome obstacles and continue moving forward.

Strategies for Effective Action

To ensure that your actions are effective and aligned with your goals, consider these strategies:

1. Prioritize Tasks: Focus on high-impact tasks that contribute directly to your goals. Prioritize these tasks to maximize your productivity and progress.

2. Create a Routine: Establish a routine that incorporates time for working on your goals. Consistent effort and dedicated time help you maintain momentum and make steady progress.

3. Leverage Resources: Utilize available resources, such as tools, technologies, and networks, to support your efforts. Resources can enhance your efficiency and effectiveness.

4. Visualize and Affirm: Continue to use visualization and affirmations to reinforce your goals and actions. These practices keep you aligned with your vision and maintain your motivation.

5. Seek Support: Surround yourself with a support network that encourages and motivates you. Collaborate with others who share your goals or offer guidance and assistance.

Exercises:

1. **Action Plan Worksheet:** Create a worksheet to outline your goals, action steps, deadlines, and resources needed. Regularly update and review your plan to stay on track.

2. **Daily Action Log:** Keep a log of your daily actions towards your goals. Reflect on your progress and identify areas for improvement or adjustment.

3. **Milestone Celebration List:** Make a list of milestones you want to achieve and how you will celebrate each one. Recognizing and celebrating your achievements reinforces your commitment and motivation.

4. **Inspirational Journal:** Maintain a journal where you record inspirations, ideas, and opportunities that arise during your manifestation journey. Review this journal regularly to stay open to new possibilities.

In the next chapter, we'll explore the concept of alignment—how to ensure that your actions, beliefs, and energy are in harmony with your goals. Alignment is crucial for attracting and manifesting your desires effectively. By understanding and applying alignment principles, you'll enhance your ability to bring your dreams to fruition and create a life that reflects your true intentions. Keep taking inspired action, and prepare to align with your vision for continued success.

Chapter 14: The Power of Alignment: Harmonizing Actions, Beliefs, and Energy

Alignment is a critical component of successful manifestation. It ensures that your actions, beliefs, and energy are all in harmony with your goals and desires. When everything is aligned, you create a powerful synergy that enhances your ability to attract and manifest your dreams. In this chapter, we'll explore what alignment means, how to achieve it, and why it's essential for turning your aspirations into reality.

What Is Alignment in Manifestation?

Alignment in manifestation refers to the state of being where your thoughts, beliefs, actions, and energy are all in harmony with your goals. It's about ensuring that every aspect of your being—mental, emotional, and physical—is working towards the same objective. When you're aligned, you create a strong and coherent signal to the universe, making it easier to attract and manifest your desires.

For instance, when I was working on manifesting a new career opportunity, alignment meant not only taking practical steps like applying for jobs and networking but also maintaining a positive mindset and belief that I deserved success. By aligning my actions, thoughts, and feelings, I was able to attract the right opportunities and achieve my career goals.

Why Alignment Is Essential

Alignment is essential because it maximizes the effectiveness of your manifestation efforts. When you're aligned:

1. Clarity and Focus: Alignment provides clarity and focus, helping you stay directed and avoid distractions. When you're clear about your goals and aligned with them, you can make better decisions and take more purposeful actions.

2. Increased Attraction: When your energy is aligned with your desires, you create a stronger magnetic field that attracts opportunities and resources. Alignment enhances your ability to draw in what you want.

3. Enhanced Motivation: Alignment keeps you motivated and energized. When your beliefs and actions are in sync, you're more likely to stay committed and enthusiastic about your goals.

4. Reduced Resistance: Misalignment often leads to internal conflict and resistance, which can hinder your progress. By aligning your thoughts, feelings, and actions, you reduce resistance and create a smoother path to achieving your desires.

5. Improved Manifestation: Alignment ensures that all parts of your manifestation process are working together harmoniously. This coherence improves your ability to manifest your goals effectively and efficiently.

How to Achieve Alignment

Achieving alignment involves aligning your thoughts, beliefs, actions, and energy with your goals. Here's how to ensure that you're in alignment:

1. Clarify Your Goals: Clearly define what you want to manifest. Understanding your goals in detail helps you align your thoughts and actions with your desires.

2. Align Your Beliefs: Ensure that your beliefs support your goals. Replace any limiting beliefs with positive affirmations that reinforce your ability to achieve your desires.

3. Take Inspired Actions: Align your actions with your goals by taking steps that move you closer to achieving them. Ensure that your daily actions reflect your commitment and intention.

4. Manage Your Energy: Pay attention to your emotional and energetic state. Engage in practices that maintain a positive and high-vibration state, such as meditation, gratitude, and self-care.

5. Visualize and Affirm: Use visualization and affirmations to keep your focus on your goals. Regularly visualize yourself achieving your desires and affirm your belief in their manifestation.

6. Reflect and Adjust: Periodically reflect on your alignment and make any necessary adjustments. If you notice any areas of misalignment, address them promptly to get back on track.

7. Stay Present: Focus on the present moment and maintain a positive mindset. Avoid dwelling on past failures or worrying about future outcomes. Staying present helps you stay aligned with your current intentions and actions.

8. Trust the Process: Trust that the universe is working with you to manifest your desires. Let go of any doubts or fears and maintain faith in the process.

Strategies for Maintaining Alignment

Maintaining alignment requires ongoing attention and effort. Here are some strategies to help you stay aligned with your goals:

1. Daily Alignment Check-In: Set aside time each day to check in with yourself and assess your alignment. Review your thoughts, beliefs, actions, and energy to ensure that everything is in harmony.

2. Alignment Journal: Keep a journal where you record your goals, beliefs, and actions. Reflect on your alignment and make note of any areas that need adjustment.

3. Alignment Rituals: Create rituals or practices that help you stay aligned, such as morning affirmations, meditation, or goal-setting sessions. Incorporate these rituals into your daily routine.

4. Seek Feedback: Share your goals and progress with a trusted mentor or coach who can provide feedback and support. External perspectives can help you identify any misalignments and make necessary adjustments.

5. Celebrate Alignment: Celebrate moments when you feel particularly aligned and successful. Acknowledging these moments reinforces your commitment and motivation.

Exercises:

1. **Alignment Visualization:** Spend a few minutes each day visualizing yourself fully aligned with your goals. Imagine your thoughts, beliefs, actions, and energy all working together harmoniously.

2. **Belief Inventory**: Take an inventory of your beliefs related to your goals. Identify any limiting beliefs and replace them with positive affirmations that support your desired outcomes.

3. **Energy Check-In:** Pay attention to your emotional and energetic state. Practice techniques to maintain a positive and balanced energy, such as deep breathing or gratitude exercises.

4. **Alignment Reflection:** Reflect on a recent experience where you felt particularly aligned with your goals. Analyze what contributed to that alignment and how you can replicate it in other areas.

In the final chapter, we'll explore the concept of celebration and gratitude. Celebrating your successes and expressing gratitude for your journey enhances the manifestation process and reinforces your positive energy. By acknowledging your achievements and appreciating the process, you'll continue to attract and manifest your desires. Embrace the power of celebration and gratitude as you complete your manifestation journey and prepare for the next chapter of your life.

Chapter 15: Celebration and Gratitude: Enhancing the Manifestation Journey

Celebration and gratitude are essential aspects of the manifestation process. They not only acknowledge your achievements but also reinforce a positive mindset and attract more abundance into your life. In this final chapter, we'll explore the importance of celebration and gratitude, how to incorporate them into your daily life, and how they contribute to the continuation of your manifestation journey.

The Importance of Celebration and Gratitude

Celebration and gratitude play a vital role in the manifestation process:

1. Reinforcing Positive Vibes: Celebrating your successes and expressing gratitude help maintain a positive vibration. This high vibration attracts more positive experiences and opportunities into your life.

2. Boosting Motivation: Recognizing and celebrating your achievements reinforces your motivation and commitment. It reminds you of your progress and encourages you to keep moving forward.

3. Enhancing Manifestation: Gratitude and celebration align your energy with abundance and success. They create an atmosphere of appreciation, which enhances your ability to manifest your desires.

4. Cultivating Joy: Celebrating and being grateful for your journey adds joy and fulfillment to your life. It shifts your focus

from what you lack to what you have, fostering a sense of contentment and satisfaction.

How to Celebrate and Practice Gratitude

Incorporating celebration and gratitude into your life involves intentional practices and mindset shifts. Here's how you can do it:

1. Celebrate Your Achievements: Take time to celebrate both big and small victories. Whether it's reaching a milestone, completing a project, or making progress towards your goals, acknowledge and reward yourself. Celebrations can be as simple as treating yourself to something special or sharing your success with loved ones.

2. Express Gratitude Daily: Practice daily gratitude by reflecting on the things you're thankful for. Keep a gratitude journal where you write down things you appreciate each day. This practice shifts your focus to positive aspects of your life and reinforces a mindset of abundance.

3. Create Gratitude Rituals: Develop rituals that help you express gratitude regularly. This could include a morning gratitude practice, a gratitude jar where you add notes of appreciation, or a gratitude meditation.

4. Share Your Gratitude: Express your gratitude to others by acknowledging their support and contributions. A simple thank you note or verbal appreciation strengthens your relationships and spreads positivity.

5. Celebrate Milestones: Set specific milestones for your goals and plan celebrations for each one. Celebrating milestones

helps you stay motivated and reinforces your commitment to your long-term objectives.

6. Reflect on Your Journey: Take time to reflect on your manifestation journey and acknowledge the progress you've made. Reflecting on your experiences and expressing gratitude for the lessons learned enhances your overall satisfaction and sense of accomplishment.

7. Maintain a Gratitude Attitude: Cultivate a gratitude attitude by focusing on the positive aspects of your daily life. Even in challenging times, look for things to be grateful for and maintain a hopeful and appreciative outlook.

Strategies for Effective Celebration and Gratitude

To make the most of celebration and gratitude, consider these strategies:

1. Create a Gratitude Ritual: Establish a daily or weekly ritual for expressing gratitude. This could be through journaling, meditation, or a gratitude-focused activity.

2. Celebrate with Intent: When celebrating, do so with intention and joy. Fully engage in the moment and savor the experience. Make celebrations meaningful and memorable.

3. Share Your Success: Share your successes and gratitude with others who have supported you. Celebrating with others fosters connection and encourages mutual support.

4. Combine Celebration with Reflection: Use celebrations as an opportunity for reflection. Consider what you've learned, how far you've come, and what you're grateful for.

5. Practice Gratitude in Adversity: Even in challenging times, find aspects to be grateful for. Practicing gratitude during difficulties helps maintain a positive mindset and supports your overall well-being.

Exercises:

1. **Gratitude Journal Exercise**: Start a gratitude journal and commit to writing down three things you're grateful for each day. Reflect on these entries regularly to reinforce a positive mindset.

2. **Celebration Planning**: Plan a celebration for reaching a specific goal or milestone. Outline how you'll celebrate and what it will mean to you. Include ways to share your celebration with others.

3. **Gratitude Reflection**: Reflect on a recent challenge and identify any positive outcomes or lessons learned. Write about these insights in your gratitude journal.

4. **Gratitude Letters**: Write letters of gratitude to people who have supported or inspired you. Express your appreciation and the impact they've had on your journey.

Conclusion

As you complete your manifestation journey, remember that celebration and gratitude are not just final steps but ongoing practices. They enhance your experience, reinforce positive energy, and attract more of what you desire into your life. By incorporating these practices, you create a vibrant and fulfilling journey, continuously attracting and manifesting your dreams.

Embrace the power of celebration and gratitude as you move forward. Appreciate your achievements, express your thanks, and maintain a positive outlook. With a grateful heart and a celebratory spirit, you'll continue to create and manifest an exceptional life filled with joy, abundance, and fulfillment. Thank you for joining me on this journey, and may your path be illuminated with success and happiness. ⟐

Also by Gavin Truesteel

BREAKING BOUNDARIES
Magic Unveiled
Finding True NORTH

Watch for more at https://67134374c7e00.site123.me/.

About the Author

About the Author: Gavin Truesteel

Gavin Truesteel is a motivational speaker, author, and personal development coach known for his captivating storytelling and practical insights on ambition, belief, and personal growth. With a deep passion for helping individuals unlock their potential, Gavin has written several books, including Breaking Boundaries: A Fable About Ambition and Belief, Magic Unveiled: A 15-Day Course on Manifestation, and Rise and Shine: The Power of Early Mornings.

Drawing from his own experiences and those of the countless people he has worked with, Gavin's work focuses on breaking through self-imposed limitations, achieving personal and professional success, and cultivating a mindset of resilience and purpose. His relatable and inspiring approach has touched the lives of many, empowering them to take control of their destinies and push beyond their boundaries.

When he's not writing or speaking at events, Gavin enjoys exploring nature, staying active, and continuously seeking new ways to grow and inspire others. Through his books and his engaging talks, Gavin remains dedicated to one mission: helping others realize that the power to change their lives lies within them.

Read more at https://67134374c7e00.site123.me/.

www.ingramcontent.com/pod-product-compliance
Lightning Source LLC
LaVergne TN
LVHW091223150826
845673LV00003B/988

9798230368809